You Are Mine: Wrestling with Faith, Hope, and Divine Love

Awakening to Belonging, Volume 1

Pride Nthabiseng Matjila-Zwane

Published by Pride Nthabiseng Matjila-Zwane, 2024.

YOU ARE MINE: WRESTLING WITH FAITH, HOPE, AND DIVINE LOVE

First edition. November 8, 2024.

Copyright © 2024 Pride Nthabiseng Matjila-Zwane.

ISBN: 979-8224107179

Written by Pride Nthabiseng Matjila-Zwane.

Table of Contents

Dedication

To my mother and grandmother,For being the pillars of my life, for showing me the true meaning of strength, resilience, and unconditional love. Your wisdom, sacrifices, and unwavering belief in me have shaped the woman I am today. You both taught me the invaluable life lessons that continue to guide me on my journey, and I carry your influence with me in every word I write. This book is as much yours as it is mine.

To my husband, Vusi,For being my rock, my confidant, and the one who gave me the courage to finally put pen to paper. Your unwavering support, encouragement, and belief in my voice have breathed life into this book. You've not only taught me the depth of love but also shown me that love has the power to inspire and transform. This book would not exist without your presence, and I am forever grateful for the role you play in my heart and in my story.

To my children,You are my blessings, my greatest joy, and the reason I rise every day. Your laughter, love, and endless curiosity fill my heart with purpose. In you, I see the future, and through you, I find my strength. This book is a reflection of the love that surrounds us, and a testament to the beautiful, unbreakable bond we share. You are my heart, and in every page, I carry you with me.

To all of you, my loves,You are mine, and I am yours. We are forever bound by the love that shapes our lives and the lessons we've shared. This book is a celebration of that love, and a reminder that we are never truly alone as long as we carry each other in our hearts.

Introduction

I've decided to write a story about myself, a novel I've always longed to create. It's taken me years to finally arrive at this point, perhaps because I wasn't sure how the story would end. I lived in hope that the conclusion would reveal itself, and now, I feel it's time to bring this journey to life. Writing about my own experiences feels daunting, but necessary. So, here I am, sharing something deeply personal, opening up about my life.

This interest to write my story began when I was around 13 years old. That was when I first felt drawn to writing. I dreamed of being an author but was consumed by fear. I would write short stories and eagerly share them with my mom and friends, and while they were impressed, I wasn't. Somehow, I always felt that my work didn't impress *me*—the person who mattered most. So, I stopped. I gave up writing for years because I didn't believe in myself enough. I convinced myself there were already too many books, too many authors—what would make my story different? What would make it worth telling?

I was afraid.

But today, I've decided to face that fear and write *my* story.

***

Chapter 1: The Beginning

Here I am, finally deciding to write my story, to speak it into existence. Perhaps it's because I'm a better storyteller than a writer, or maybe there's no real difference. All I know is that I have stories within me that need to be told—stories that have shaped my understanding of the world and my place in it. I'm not sure if anyone will be interested in what I have to share, but I'll start by developing a few chapters and see where this journey leads. Hopefully, someone, somewhere, will connect with these words, will feel something familiar or profound.

The title of my book is *You are mine*. Why did I choose this title? I don't know exactly, but it feels right. It speaks to the idea that I am my own person. I belong to myself, but not only myself alone. Despite the influences that others have in our lives, no one knows us better than we know ourselves. We spend the most time with ourselves, and we bear the greatest responsibility for shaping who we are.

So, how do I see myself? What do I feel when I look in the mirror?

It's funny how much I've changed over the years. Growing up, I was mostly confident. I had dark, curly hair and beautiful caramel skin, with dimples that would light up my smile. People often complimented me on my bright smile and my eyes—slightly almond-shaped, which some said looked almost like those of someone from far a different world. But still, beneath all those compliments, there were insecurities. There were things I didn't feel confident about, things people said that chipped away at how I saw myself.

I was born on the 21st of April, 1990, in a small village, the first child of my parents. My great-grandmother's home was where it all began. It was a compact situation because, at the time, my grandmother hadn't built a house yet; she was living in Tembisa, where she worked as a helper in the kitchens for three white families. With the little money she earned, she took care of her children. My mother was raised by her grandparents, living among ten other cousins who were also being raised by their grandparents because their parents had gone away to seek a better life to support the family.

As a child, I wasn't exposed much to these things because I was too young. These were stories told to me later, piecing together my past from childhood photos and memories. My parents met while they were both in high school. My father was raised by his uncle and aunt, having been abandoned by his mother. The life he lived seemed filled with pain that only he understood. You could see it in the way he spoke and sometimes in his eyes, which held fear, doubt, and anxiety, as if he were unsure he was going in the right direction. The absence of his mother had a profound impact on him, creating a sense of loss that perhaps drew him to my mother.

When they fell in love, it was a time of innocence. My mother saw a pure heart in him, even as he was a child without a stable home. Everyone in his family tried to give him a life he needed—shelter, food, comfort—but it just didn't seem fulfilling to him. I've never been one to tell another person's story, believing that there are always different versions. Stories are better told by the owner because they touch on important elements and memories that only that person can access.

At 19, my mother became pregnant with me. My father, for some reason, ended up without a place to go, so my mother asked her grandparents if he could live with them. She wanted to give him a sense of belonging. With their permission, my father came to live with them. By then, my mother's older brother was working in a different province, her other brother was also away, so the household consisted of my great-grandparents, my mother, and my father.

Nine months later, I was born at a local government clinic. Living in the village meant one had to walk about 5 kilometers to get to the nearest clinic. So, my mother and her grandmother walked to the clinic while she was in labor. Even in those harsh conditions, it was normal for them, as it was the only way they knew. My mother recounted that I was born on a Saturday morning at 6:00 AM, and I had a cord wrapped around my neck. Thankfully, I managed to survive.

My great-grandmother had given birth to nine children, with three surviving at the time of her passing. Losing her was definitely a difficult time in my mother's life. Yet, in her grief, my mother found solace in knowing she had a daughter who could fill the void left by her grandmother. I believe my great-grandmother was the kind of woman my mother aspired to become. Although my great-grandparents didn't work, relying mostly on farming and livestock to sustain their lives, they managed to provide a strong foundation for our family.

Life wasn't easy. My family lived through the apartheid era in South Africa, where opportunities were limited for Black people. While he lived with my grandmother in KwaNdebele, my uncle sometimes had to hide under the bed when the authorities came looking for young boys. Such experiences were traumatic, and while I was born during that era, I felt its impact through the stories shared by my family.

When I was about three or four years old, my grandmother built a home a few meters away from my great-grandparents' house. This land was gifted to her by her father after she couldn't get a house in another area due to discrimination. She quickly found a way to ensure her children's safety, leading to the construction of a two-room house where my parents lived which they later moved into a bigger house. My uncle lived there first before my parents followed. My father was often unemployed, taking on odd jobs, while my mother was in school learning handiwork and sewing.

I believe that was the sacrifice parents had to make—trusting others to care for their child while they worked. I was raised by the village, as the saying goes. Parents often had to work away from home, leaving their children with relatives or family friends. My upbringing was greatly influenced by various grandmothers. I witnessed their struggles as they faced old age and illness. One family friend's grandmother had, what I now understand to be Parkinson's disease, and I remember her trembling hands. Even though I didn't understand what was happening, it was a part of life that left a mark on me. I often questioned why these strong women who had raised me would sometimes struggle silently. It made me realize how deeply our community was affected by their circumstances, yet they continued with life as if nothing was wrong.

In the midst of all these experiences, my childhood was also marked by a harsh environment. Growing up in an African household, comments about my appearance were often blunt and sometimes brutal, even if they weren't meant to hurt. I grew up a little chubby, which led to constant comments about my weight. This made me feel flawed and like there was something inherently wrong with me, as if I wasn't good enough. I began to believe that my weight was why people didn't like me or why I struggled to fit in.

That desire to fit in turned me into a people pleaser, which damaged me more than anything else. I made the wrong friends, seeking validation from the wrong people. I wanted to be accepted and feel like I belonged. But even when I thought I had found genuine connections, something would always change. I'd be cast aside, left wondering why.

One of my first experiences of feeling betrayed by friends happened in primary school. I transferred to a new pre-primary school mid-year, hopeful because I knew a few kids from the neighborhood. At first, it seemed like they wanted to be my friends because I was pretty, and I naively thought that was enough. But it didn't take long for me to realize their interest wasn't genuine. I was heartbroken, not because I was left out, but because I had offered them my genuine self, only to have it rejected.

That rejection hurt. It cut deep, especially when those I thought were friends became the very people who bullied me in primary school, turning my world upside down. I didn't know who to lean on. This was because my mother was strict, raising me on her own after my father left. She was my rock but also distant, too caught up in her own survival to notice my pain. When my father left, it shattered something in me, though I didn't recognize it at the time. I wanted her to fight for their marriage, to keep our family together, but that wasn't in her control.

I grew up in a household filled with tension, with arguments and violence simmering just beneath the surface. Even though I could hear the fights, the anger spilling out behind closed doors, I taught myself to tune it out, believing that prayer would somehow fix everything. As a little girl, I would kneel by my bed and ask God to make it all go away.

I remember one particular time when my father didn't come home for weeks. My mother, stressed and anxious, finally opened up to me about how desperate the situation had become. We were running out of food, and there was no way for her to reach him. This was before cell phones, so the only way to contact him was to call his workplace using a payphone. The chances of reaching him were slim, and she felt helpless. So did I.

I retreated to my room, knelt down, and prayed harder than I ever had, asking God to bring my father home, to fill our cupboards with food. Miraculously, He answered. That very afternoon, as I looked out the window, there was my father, walking up the driveway after being gone for so long. That moment cemented my belief in the power of prayer, the hope that someone was listening, that things could somehow change.

But soon after, I discovered that my father's homecoming wasn't a sign of improvement. It was the same old pattern. He would leave again, and the cycle continued. I began to see the weariness in my mother's eyes. I was her support, her confidante. I didn't want to put more weight on her shoulders, but I was also yearning for a sense of normalcy and safety.

For a long time, I suppressed my feelings. I learned to ignore the ache in my chest, the sorrow that loomed large when I thought about my father. I began to believe that maybe my mother was right, that I didn't need him to be happy. Yet, deep down, I longed for that connection. I felt torn between loyalty to my mother and a desire for my father's love.

This duality began to shape my perception of relationships. I was yearning for love but afraid of vulnerability. I sought out friendships, believing they could fill that void. Little did I know, that pursuit would lead me into toxic relationships, where I continuously sought validation. I often found myself entangled in unhealthy dynamics, feeling unworthy of love or respect. It was a painful journey, but through soul-searching and forgiveness, I learned to embrace self-love and realize my worth.

So, this is where my story begins. It's a journey filled with struggles and triumphs, and I hope you'll walk alongside me as I unravel the layers of my past. It's not just a story of pain but one of resilience, of discovering who I am beneath all the hurt, anger, and confusion. As I write, I aim to honor those who came before me, the women who shaped me, and the lessons learned through pain.

With each word, I hope to inspire others to embrace their own journeys, to find healing in their stories. This is just the beginning, and I'm excited to see where this path will lead.

***

Chapter 2: Wrestling with Faith

I decided to start with my identity because, in many ways, it has shaped who I am. But more than that, this book is about my faith—the core of who I am—and how it has brought me to this point. I'm not sure if I chose to be a Christian or if it was simply thrust upon me. When you're born into a family with a specific belief, you're handed that faith without question. It becomes the framework through which you view the world, your lens of understanding. But do we truly grasp what we are given? Not always. Sometimes, the layers of meaning behind the faith we inherit remain hidden until we start questioning them ourselves.

Growing up, I accepted Christianity because it was all I knew. It was the atmosphere I breathed, the backdrop of my childhood. But as I got older, I started to question what I had been taught. I remember moments when doubt would creep in—when I would find myself asking difficult questions about my faith. I specifically remember questioning the existence of Jesus, or rather, struggling to understand why He was so special. Even if I didn't doubt His existence, I couldn't wrap my mind around why He was chosen—why He was so favored by God. Why Him? Why was He the one sent to earth to die for all of us?

At times, the whole story felt abstract, almost surreal. I mean, how could someone sacrifice their life for people they didn't even know? That level of selflessness seemed impossible to me. We live in a world where survival often means looking out for yourself, where people's actions are driven by self-preservation, self-interest. So the idea that someone could willingly give up their life for others, without hesitation, left me feeling confused and frustrated. It made me wonder: "Could I ever do that? Could I ever be that selfless?"

I found myself grappling with this question for years. It wasn't just about faith—it was about how I saw myself. I couldn't imagine making such a sacrifice, especially not after having experienced the uglier sides of humanity. You see, my story—like many others—isn't just about faith.

It's also about pain, trauma, and survival. And that's where the tension lies. How could I understand selfless love when, in my own life, I had been exposed to betrayal, violation, and hurt?

This part of my story is one I don't often talk about. To be honest, I've avoided it for years, even though it's shaped so much of who I am. I don't know how to write this chapter of my life, but something tells me that sharing it may help someone else. Maybe it will bring healing, not only for me but for others who have experienced something similar. I'm not sure if I've completely healed from it or if I'm still in the process of seeking healing and restoration. I only know that a part of me was taken away that I can never get back.

It's even harder because I've allowed my mind to block out some of the memories. I think that's what trauma does—it makes you push things so deep inside that you almost forget they exist. Almost. But the pain has a way of resurfacing, reminding you of what you've been through. I never wanted to associate myself with that experience, never wanted to think of myself as a victim. I always wanted to be strong, to overcome, to be a victor. But this one experience—this violation—it made me drown. Even as I tried to find ways to cope by writing in my journal as I grew up, the scars remained.

When you're a child, you don't understand what is happening to you. I was six years old when it happened. Six. Barely old enough to comprehend the world around me, let alone the dark corners of humanity. I was violated by someone I trusted—a close family friend. It wasn't something I could even process at that age. I didn't understand why this was happening or what it even meant. All I knew was that it hurt. And that hurt stayed with me, deeply etched into my memory, no matter how hard I tried to forget.

I didn't talk about it. Not to my friends, not to my family. This was a secret I kept for years, hidden behind layers of shame and confusion. It wasn't just about the act itself, but about what it made me feel—dirty, disgusting, like I had done something wrong. I would question myself:

"Did I do something to deserve this? Did I put myself in this situation?" Maybe I walked the wrong way, said the wrong thing, or dressed in a way that invited it. Those thoughts haunted me. Growing up in an African household, you are taught to carry yourself a certain way—to sit, walk, and behave modestly. There's a lot of emphasis on how a girl should act, and I wondered if I had somehow failed in that.

But there's another layer to it. In our culture, you are also taught to respect your elders. It doesn't matter if they are related to you or not—if they are older, you are expected to listen to them, obey them. That's the way it was in the village where I grew up. You don't question an elder's authority. So when this elder—this family friend—betrayed my trust, I was left completely confused. How could someone I was supposed to respect do something so wrong? How was I supposed to reconcile these two conflicting ideas—respect for elders and the need to protect myself?

I suppose the betrayal shook my foundation. It wasn't just physical—it was emotional and spiritual. It wasn't until much later that I understood how deeply that moment had impacted me. It changed how I viewed trust, love, and even God. How could God allow something like this to happen? How could He let a child—innocent, vulnerable—be violated? How could someone who was supposed to protect me be the one who harmed me?

These are questions I wrestled with for years, questions that drove me further into anger and resentment. I started questioning everything, even my own worth. Was I worthy of love, of protection? If I wasn't perfect, did that mean I wasn't worthy of God's love? I wanted to be loved by Him so badly, almost desperately. I wanted to believe that there was a reason for my existence—a purpose beyond the pain. But in the midst of all the confusion, I wondered if I was even worthy of that love.

I tried to make sense of it by turning to faith, by trying to be "good enough" for God. But what did that even mean? I didn't know. I just knew that I wanted to believe there had to be something more—a greater being, a bigger purpose. The world was too magnificent, too complex to have been created by mere humans. There had to be a Creator, right? But why did this Creator allow so much pain, so much injustice?

In school, I joined the choir. I'm not sure if I was a good singer—I still don't know. But I found myself there, singing soprano, representing my school at competitions, assemblies, and morning prayers. Every time I tried to hit those high notes, my voice would crack. I didn't believe I was good enough. The other kids had better voices than mine, but still, there I was, singing praises to God. And yet, I didn't understand. Why did God need so much praise? Why was He so insatiable for it? It didn't make sense to me.

The more I sang, the more I questioned. The more I questioned, the more I struggled with my faith. And then, something strange happened—something that I still don't fully understand. It started in primary school. I began seeing things—reflections, almost like shadows of people who had passed on. I remember when a girl from our school passed away, and I could swear I saw her. I thought it was normal, that everyone could see what I saw. But I quickly realized that wasn't the case.

Seeing these shadows, these reflections, made me curious. What happens when we die? Where do we go? I became obsessed with death, even though it terrified me. The thought of my spirit separating from my body was suffocating. I didn't want to experience it, even as an abstract idea. But the more I thought about it, the more questions arose. What happens to the soul? Is there life after death? And if so, why are some people taken so soon while others live long, full lives?

The anger I had inside me grew, especially when I saw young children—innocent, pure—losing their lives. How could a loving, merciful God allow that? How could He let children die before they even had a chance to live? It didn't make sense. I grew up seeing people who weren't good—people who were greedy, envious, harmful—living long lives, while good, kind-hearted people were taken too soon. It felt like an injustice, an imbalance that I couldn't reconcile with the idea of a loving God.

I would look at the world around me and see the good people struggling. How could this be fair? How could a God who supposedly loved us all equally allow such injustice? I started to question more than just the world—I started questioning myself, my faith, and whether I could ever really trust in anything. It felt as if the foundations I had been raised on were slowly crumbling. The teachings about love, kindness, and divine justice didn't align with what I saw around me, especially in my own life.

That betrayal—the violation I experienced at six years old—left a scar that never truly healed. I carried the weight of that moment through my adolescence and into

adulthood. It affected how I saw myself, how I interacted with others, and how I viewed the world. It wasn't just a physical wound—it was emotional, mental, and spiritual. And even now, I still wrestle with it.

Was I worthy of love, of protection, of God's grace? Could I ever fully heal from that experience? These are the questions that have shaped my journey, my faith, and my identity. They are the questions that have driven me to search for answers, to find meaning in a world that often feels chaotic and unjust.

But through it all, I have learned one thing: Healing is a process. It's not linear. It doesn't happen all at once. And while I may never fully understand why certain things happened to me, I know that my story has value. Sharing it, as difficult as it may be, is a step toward healing—for me and perhaps for others who have gone through something similar.

I may never have all the answers, but I've learned to keep searching, to keep questioning, and to keep believing that, despite the pain, there is still hope. There is still love. And most importantly, there is still faith.

***

Chapter 3: The Journey of Growth

I graduated from primary school in 2002, around twelve years old, soon to turn thirteen. This marked the end of my childhood and the beginning of a new chapter—my entry into adolescence. It was a time of significant transition, both physically and emotionally, as I moved from the familiar world of childhood into the unknown terrain of teenage life. Up until that point, I had been deeply attuned to a mysterious, almost spiritual world that felt disconnected from the physical realities I was beginning to face. But as I entered this new phase of life, the world around me became more real, more tangible.

Adolescence brought with it emotional changes that I wasn't fully prepared for. I began to grapple with questions about my identity—who I was and how I fit into the world around me. My body was changing, my emotions were all over the place, and I found myself dealing with pressures I didn't fully understand. I was entering the journey of growth, but it was confusing. Transitioning into adolescence, becoming a teenager, you start learning new things, and suddenly the world seems like a more complex place.

I was surrounded by friends and peers who were navigating this stage of life in their own ways. Some were dating, exploring relationships for the first time, and it felt like everyone around me was moving forward in life while I was stuck trying to figure things out. Peer pressure became a constant presence, with friends experimenting with smoking and other behaviors. It felt like there was an expectation to fit in, to participate in things I wasn't comfortable with. The perception of intimacy, which had been introduced to me in such a harmful way, left me conflicted. Should I accept it? Reject it? I didn't know.

For the longest time, I felt like I didn't have a voice when it came to things like copulation. It seemed like it held power over me, something I could never control. I hadn't chosen it, it had been forced upon me. Because it was introduced to me when I was not ready for it, I felt like

I had no say. I couldn't make decisions for myself when it came to these things. The lines were blurred, and I was lost, unsure of who to turn to for guidance.

Peer pressure only made things worse. Teenagers would talk openly about their experiences, and when you didn't participate, you were made to feel stupid or left out. It was as if not indulging in these things made you seem like you were pretending to be better than them. It was difficult to stand my ground when I didn't even fully understand what I was standing for. Looking back, I realize how unhealthy it was. Peer pressure often stems from the environment we are raised in, and for many of my peers, that environment was dysfunctional. Growing up in homes filled with abuse or neglect leaves a lasting impact on how you interact with the world.

Around this time, my parents' divorce had occurred, three years earlier, and the emotional impact of that was still very fresh. My father's departure from our family left me feeling abandoned, confused, and yearning for a sense of love and security. It felt like a part of my identity was ripped away when he left. My parents had been together for as long as I could remember, and I had never imagined that love could end. In my young mind, love was eternal, something that lasted forever, and watching my parents separate shattered that belief.

My father's remarriage and the creation of a new life, a new family, left me with a profound sense of loss. It felt like he had moved on without us, leaving my mother and me behind. That abandonment weighed heavily on me, making me question my worth. Who was I without him? Was I even lovable? My once secure home had become a place filled with sorrow, and my mother, who had always been a stay-at-home mom, now had to step up and become both mother and provider. It was the first time I saw her struggle, and it left a deep impression on me.

My mother was resilient, though. She fought hard to provide for us, even when it meant learning new skills like braiding hair to bring in some income. She wanted to go back to school, learn handiwork, and eventually start her own business. Watching her navigate these challenges taught me the value of hard work and determination. Our life in the village was simple—no paved roads, no running water, and we used a pit toilet. But even in those humble circumstances, I didn't feel deprived. Life in the village, despite its simplicity, had a certain richness.

I remember how, during power outages, we'd sit around the table with candles lit, sharing stories for hours. Those moments felt precious. The absence of modern distractions allowed us to connect on a deeper level, and even though we didn't have much, we had each other. My cousins, who often visited us during the holidays, would join in. Despite coming from different backgrounds, we always shared a deep bond, one that transcended our circumstances.

My grandmother's role in assisting with my upbringing also had a profound impact on me. She was a quiet force of strength, working as a domestic worker to provide for her family. Like my mother, she had no husband by her side, but she built a home for her children through sheer willpower. She never complained, never spoke of the burden she carried, and remained humble and kind throughout it all. Her strength was both silent and immense, and it shaped how I viewed resilience and determination.

My grandmother was also deeply spiritual, often praying with a white candle lit by her side. She believed in the power of faith and taught me that even in the toughest times, hope could carry you through. Her faith was unwavering, and that, in turn, gave her the strength to keep going, no matter what life threw her way. It was a lesson I held close to my heart and would carry with me throughout my own life.

This hope and resilience were also deeply ingrained in my mother. She was determined to create a better life for us, so when the opportunity came for her to go to university, she didn't hesitate. My uncle offered to help her, and she enrolled at the University of South Africa. Though she initially wanted to become a teacher, her studies eventually led her to social work, which became her passion.

For four years, my mother worked tirelessly to earn her degree. By the time she graduated, I was already in high school, and I couldn't have been prouder. She became the first woman in our family to graduate from university. Her accomplishment was monumental, not just for her but for all of us. It wasn't just about education; it was about breaking barriers, about showing me that with hard work and perseverance, anything was possible.

As I moved through my teenage years, I became more aware of the world outside my family and village. School activities like debate competitions helped build my confidence. One standout experience was competing in an Afrikaans debate against students from other schools. It was intimidating, especially coming from a small village where such opportunities were rare. But participating in that debate helped me realize that I had a voice, and that my opinions mattered. It wasn't just about winning—it was about finding my voice, standing up for myself, and believing in my ability to make a difference.

At the same time, I continued to struggle with questions of faith. My mother's and grandmother's strong belief in God had always been a source of comfort for them, but I found myself questioning it. How could a loving God allow so much suffering? Poverty, loss, and hardship were all around me, and it was difficult to reconcile that with the idea of a merciful, benevolent deity. But no matter how much I questioned, I always found myself drawn back to the concept of God. Faith was a part of me, even when I didn't fully understand it.

As I grew older, my understanding of love also evolved. My parents' divorce had left me confused about what love really was. Could it last? Was it something that could fade, like it had for my parents? I wasn't sure. But as I watched my mother and grandmother love and care for me unconditionally, I began to realize that love wasn't just about romance. It wasn't about grand gestures or fairytale endings. Sometimes, love was quiet. It was about showing up, day after day, even when things were tough.

Through the struggles and heartache, I learned that love isn't perfect. It's messy and complicated, but real love, the kind my mother and grandmother showed me, endures. It survives the hardships and disappointments, and it stays, even when everything else seems to fall apart.

***

Chapter 4: Breaking the Silence: Reclaiming Myself

In this chapter, I share memories of when I first began dating, a time that was both innocent and filled with uncertainty. At the age of 14, I found myself navigating emotions I had never felt before, unaware of how much these early experiences would shape me. At that time, I had very little understanding of romantic feelings or relationships. The first time I saw a boy I liked, I remember vividly how my heart raced, and I felt butterflies in my stomach. It was a strange, exhilarating sensation, one that left me confused and excited all at once.

When I confided in my friends, they explained to me that what I was feeling was called a "crush." Despite liking him, I was too scared to let him know. Every time he tried to talk to me, I would run away, overcome by fear and anxiety. It seemed easier to avoid him than face the possibility of rejection or, even worse, disapproval from the adults in my life. I was particularly concerned about what my mother would say. She had always emphasized the importance of focusing on school and avoiding distractions, especially boys. "Books before boys," she would say, a mantra she often repeated.

My mother was strict and held high expectations for me, especially regarding my education. She believed my success in school would open doors for me, and she didn't want anything to interfere with that. I didn't want to disappoint her or tarnish my image as the "good girl." I was known for being the one who got straight A's, followed the rules, and did everything by the book. Any deviation from that path felt like a betrayal of who I was supposed to be. Despite my fears and inner conflict, I eventually gave in to the boy's advances. He told me he cared about me, and I thought I felt the same way. I was still trying to understand my emotions, not yet grasping what it meant for someone to show interest in me.

Our "relationship," if it could even be called that, was short-lived. Almost as soon as it began, I changed schools, which led to an unexpected twist in my teenage love life. At my new school, I met someone else—someone who, unbeknownst to me at the time, was his cousin. Looking back, it felt like a betrayal, but at the time, I was just a young girl trying to make sense of relationships and feelings. My inexperience and innocence led me to stumble through those early encounters.

This new relationship was also brief, never developing into anything serious. My mother's protective nature meant that I wasn't allowed out much, leaving little opportunity for us to spend time together. The dynamic of our "relationship" mostly consisted of stolen glances and whispered conversations between classes. I never fully understood what was happening, but deep down, I was searching for something—connection, perhaps. At that age, I longed for closeness, a feeling that might fill the void left by my father's absence.

My father's departure had created a gaping emotional hole in my life. Dating, in my teenage mind, seemed like a way to explore love, intimacy, and care—things I felt I had lost. But those experiences also brought confusion and pressure. I didn't know how to navigate these emotions, especially since I was still carrying the weight of a painful childhood experience—something I hadn't shared with anyone, not even my mother.

Growing up, I faced moments of blurred boundaries around intimacy, particularly due to sexual violence I experienced when I was young. As I transitioned into my teenage years, this left me feeling confused. The emotional wounds from the past made it difficult to approach dating or romantic feelings with clarity. I found myself in situations where I struggled to say no, even though my mind and body were not ready for the kinds of expectations that seemed to come with being in a relationship.

I often felt judged by those around me, even though they couldn't have known what I had been through. There was a constant internal dialogue: did people see through me? Did they sense I was no longer the same innocent girl? The shame and confusion about my past made it difficult to navigate the conversations about intimacy that started to arise in my teenage relationships.

I felt immense pressure when boys asked personal questions like, "Are you a virgin?" It was a question loaded with complexity for me. If I said yes, I felt the pressure to engage in intimacy, because it seemed like everyone else was doing it. If I said no, I worried it would lead to more uncomfortable questions. In my mind, I felt unable to open up about my past. I doubted that the boys I dated, who were themselves still immature, could understand the emotional and psychological weight I was carrying. Their focus seemed to be on what they wanted, not on understanding my struggles or respecting my boundaries.

This added to my confusion and reluctance to engage in any intimate acts at a young age. It also made it difficult for me to seek guidance from elders, teachers, or even my mother. Growing up in a strict African household, where the rules were rigid and non-negotiable, only made matters worse. Sometimes, I was accused of things I hadn't done and even punished for perceived wrongdoings. I wasn't allowed to talk back to my parents or defend myself, which eroded the trust between us. With no room to explain or be heard, I became even more isolated in dealing with my internal struggles.

This internal conflict shaped the way I viewed myself and my relationships. I didn't understand why certain situations made me uncomfortable or why I struggled to fully trust others. There was a tension between the image of the "good girl" I was expected to be and the complex emotions I was dealing with beneath the surface. I lacked the tools to address these emotions, so I did what I thought I was supposed to do: I stayed quiet, kept my head down, and tried to focus on school.

It was during school that I finally began to find some of the answers I had been searching for. We had a life orientation class that covered topics about growing up and understanding our bodies. One day, our teacher introduced us to a book that explained the changes we were experiencing during adolescence. I borrowed the book over the holidays and read it from cover to cover. For the first time, I felt like I had a clearer understanding of myself.

The book was eye-opening. It helped me realize that my feelings and experiences were part of growing up. It gave me a sense of validation, helping me let go of some of the shame and confusion from the brutal violation that had followed me for so long. It was a turning point in my journey toward self-awareness and self-acceptance. Armed with this newfound understanding, I made a decision that would mark a significant shift in my life: I broke up with my boyfriend.

It wasn't a dramatic breakup, but it was a necessary one for me. Ending the relationship symbolized something deeper: my decision to reclaim my sense of self-worth. I realized I deserved more than a relationship that left me feeling small and uncertain. I chose to focus on my education and my future, redirecting my energy toward my goals rather than fleeting affections. This decision marked the beginning of a new chapter in my life.

That choice changed everything. It wasn't just about ending a relationship—it was about taking back control of my life and my decisions. For so long, I had felt confused and lost, unsure of how to navigate relationships or how to handle the emotional scars from my past. Breaking up with my boyfriend was a step toward healing and finding myself. It was a declaration that I would no longer allow my worth to be defined by others.

My early dating experiences, though filled with confusion and pain, taught me an invaluable lesson: I am in control of my own life and choices. No one else defines my value or my future. I deserve respect and dignity, and I will not settle for anything less. While those early relationships may have been brief, the lessons they imparted were profound. I learned that love—at least the kind of love I wanted—couldn't be rushed or forced. It required a deep sense of self-awareness and a strong foundation of self-respect.

As I reflect on those years, I see how much I've grown. I was a young girl trying to understand the world and my place in it, but I had a desire to learn and grow. The experiences I went through, while difficult, helped shape me into the woman I am today. They taught me resilience, strength, and the importance of self-love.

Looking back, I also appreciate the role my mother played in my life. Her emphasis on education and self-respect laid the groundwork for the decisions I made later on. Though I often struggled with her strictness, I now understand that she was preparing me for the challenges I would face in life. She taught me that my worth wasn't dependent on anyone else's approval.

In the end, those early dating experiences were about more than just romantic relationships—they were about understanding myself, my boundaries, and what I deserved in life. They were the first steps on a long journey toward self-discovery and empowerment. For that, I am grateful, even for the painful lessons, because they made me who I am today.

***

Chapter 5: Emerging from Shadows: My High School Journey of Growth and Identity

In 2005, I started high school at fifteen, and life became more interesting. Attending a new school for the first time meant using transportation to get there. It wasn't a prestigious institution, but in our community, it was regarded as a good school. Gaining admission was challenging; you had to be smart or present yourself impressively to seize the opportunity. While I was in middle school, I participated in debate competitions and caught the attention of a teacher from this new school. He was impressed by our performance against high schoolers and suggested that after we graduated, we should come to his school.

I found myself at a school far from my village, and the stereotypes surrounding children from the village weighed heavily on us. We were not immediately welcomed by the other students, who came from better homes. Their parents were teachers, principals, or worked for the government, while many of us were raised by single parents, often struggling to make ends meet. It was daunting to step into a place where others seemed to lead better lives.

Having the opportunity to attend such a school was intimidating, and I worried about whether I would float or sink in this new environment. But one thing was certain: I wanted to make something of my life. My mother made significant sacrifices for me, and I was determined to make her proud. Tired of being the center of attention, I decided to avoid extracurricular activities. I didn't want to represent the school or attract attention, especially since I was already bullied for being favored by teachers. The other students viewed me as a "pick-me" child, and I didn't want to step on their toes in what felt like their territory.

I focused on my schoolwork, but I couldn't escape the bullying. I wore a long skirt that went below my knees, while they wore skirts that went above their knees. I was labeled the "church girl." It wasn't easy, and I couldn't even think about dating, as I felt completely out of place. The boys at this school didn't seem interested in me, and I often wondered how I fit into their world.

On the academic side, I faced new challenges. I was now studying accounting; I was doing economics and other subjects that were becoming increasingly difficult. In my first term, I excelled in mathematics and accounting, earning a 98%. I was celebrated in class, but as the months passed, I began to struggle. The math became more complex, and I found it hard to cope, especially with the language barrier; my teacher, who was Nigerian, pronounced some words in ways that confused me.

Eventually, I failed mathematics in the second term, and I was devastated. I couldn't turn to my mother for help; she wasn't good at math, and I couldn't afford a tutor. I stared at graphs and shapes, feeling as if I were looking at a foreign language. I eventually surrendered, resigned to the possibility of failure. Despite my efforts, I failed mathematics again in the third term.

But I knew I had to pull myself together. I told myself I needed to get at least a 50% to progress to the next grade. Thankfully, I passed mathematics in the fourth term, moving on to Grade 11 at sixteen. I was nervous; things were only going to get harder.

As I entered this new grade, I felt increasingly isolated. Friends I had come with from my village were making new friends, leaving me behind. The transition was painful, and I didn't understand what had changed. I found a new friend, an older girl from a boarding school. She was experimenting with various aspects of life, and being exposed to someone who identified as bisexual during such a confusing time sparked my curiosity. I wanted to understand what that meant, even though I knew it was something my mother and my community disapproved of.

What I learned about her was that she had also endured hardships, and it was evident that our experiences shaped who we became. There was a connection, a sense of understanding, even though she didn't know my story. For the first time, I felt like I wasn't alone. I had experienced violation, my parents' divorce, and the turmoil of wanting something different in a world I didn't fully understand. I wanted to believe in the existence of good people and true love.

I was intrigued by older couples who had stood the test of time. How had they made it work? I wanted that kind of lasting relationship, even at sixteen. My desire transcended academic success; I sought a deeper understanding of life's purpose. I recognized that while we often chase material things like money and acceptance, there are essential aspects of existence that go beyond the physical realm.

Though I was doing well in school, something was missing. I was not fulfilled. Even as I engaged with my faith, I often felt disconnected from the church. The preacher recited the Bible, but his interpretation seemed superficial. It felt as though many were merely imitating others without a genuine understanding of the messages being preached. Some congregants would leave for other churches that were essentially the same but offered different interpretations of faith.

This inconsistency left me questioning. Were we truly in touch with who we were meant to be? I longed for answers and deeper connections, not just the surface-level understanding I often encountered.

I finished my matric in 2007. While I passed, I didn't perform to the best of my abilities; I was emotionally exhausted and ready to let go of the pressure of perfection. I was tired of pretending to be something I wasn't. I took my 60% and enrolled in university to study accounting, hoping to prove something to my family. But deep down, I questioned whether this was what I truly wanted.

My first semester was manageable, but the second semester was a different story. I struggled immensely, feeling inadequate. Seeking fulfillment, I found myself pregnant at eighteen during my first year at university. It was a shocking time in my life. I felt emotionally and psychologically unprepared for motherhood. How could I care for a child when I couldn't even take care of myself?

I knew that the unstable relationship I was in would not provide a healthy environment for a child. I had to reclaim my life and accept that being a single mother wasn't a curse. If I focused on my child, I could give them more than I could ever give myself. As terrified as I was, this realization opened my eyes and led me to reconsider the decisions I was making in my life.

***

Chapter 6: Embracing Change

Now I'm in Mamelodi, having moved from the village with my mother, who had just secured her first job as a lecturer at a prestigious university. This was a proud moment for us because it was the first time, after a long period, that we experienced such a significant blessing. For once, we didn't have to feel like a burden or that we didn't deserve good things. Incredibly and miraculously, due to her hard work and her compelling story, her lecturer and supervisor found her inspirational and encouraged her to apply for the position. They believed she could potentially secure employment.

Having grown up in a village in a small town, being around these knowledgeable people was intimidating for her. But she went for it, applied for the position, and, incredibly enough, she got the job. Our lives changed completely. She purchased her first home in Mamelodi, and that's how we came to live there.

After a year in Mamelodi, I fell pregnant. When I gave birth to my daughter, my mother stepped up to help me raise her, as the father was out of the picture. Even though I didn't know what I was doing, the support of my family helped me not give up on life. They encouraged me to go back to university. Here I was, struggling in accounting while raising a child and having taken a gap year to care for an infant. That was very difficult, and I struggled a lot. One moment, I was registered for classes, and when it came time to write my exams, I would get panic attacks and wouldn't go to the exam. I just wasn't performing well. At one point, I even took another gap year because my daughter fell ill, and I had to take care of her.

Prioritizing being a student and a mother was incredibly challenging, and I think that's when I found myself seeking something deeper. It felt like whatever had been following me all these years had finally found me. It caught up with me during quiet, emotional hours when I needed comfort and compassion. I call this chapter "When the Creator Found

Me" because I felt like I had been running away from Him or Her all my life. I could sense something chasing me, wanting to embrace me, but I was fleeing, perhaps out of fear and feelings of unworthiness, or simply not understanding what it was and why it wanted me so much.

Sometimes, we might feel like we are seeking redemption, but really, it is redemption that has been seeking us all along. For me, redemption found me when I was alone in my room, caring for my baby. For some reason, I found myself weeping on the floor, longing for a big embrace, as if I knew there was a presence meant to envelop me in warmth and love.

I started watching a religious TV program that broadcast sermons and began listening to gospel music. For some reason, I found healing in it. It wasn't planned; it felt like a relationship. You know how they say love is blind? It felt like that. I just felt this presence that had been following me finally catch me.

I watched these shows every single day, seven days a week. My mother was not impressed because it meant I was neglecting my studies, but she couldn't understand that I couldn't fight it, even if I tried. I would be in my room in the middle of the night, having just put my baby to sleep, planning to study, but I couldn't do it. I was overwhelmed by this feeling. I would feel immensely emotional, start crying, and pray for no apparent reason. I knew this was something beyond me, and I couldn't fight it. I didn't want to fight it because it felt peaceful and comforting, like something I was lacking. I didn't know what it was or have a name for it, but I knew the sermons I listened to called it God, faith, religion, the Holy Spirit, or Jesus Christ.

Whether I wanted to name it didn't matter; my perception of who God is to me is personal. It doesn't matter if He is male or female, black or white. I just knew that this great feeling I experienced inside was greater than anything I had ever felt before, and I didn't want to let it go. I didn't care if I was failing in school by spending all this time watching these sermons, listening to music, or reading the Bible. I felt like God wanted my time and attention, and when He wanted it, I would set aside my books and focus on that, as it was fulfilling.

I felt like an outcast in my family because everyone else was striving and graduating. Here I was, struggling to complete a course while raising a baby at a young age. I spent my 21st birthday raising my child, but ironically, I was just grateful for the blessing. I felt she was my gift from God because had I not had her, I wouldn't have had the time to give God my attention. Now I was free, available, and there were no distractions. She saved me, and I could never see her as a disturbance or interference in my life because she came at a time when I truly needed that connection with God.

I'm grateful for those moments because, without them, I was on the verge of giving up. I attempted suicide many times without my family's knowledge because I felt it was pointless for me to still be alive. I didn't understand the significance of my existence. I was rejected by my father and thought I could never be anything special. My mother was living her life and thriving in her career, and I didn't want to be a distraction to that. She deserved this moment to shine, to enjoy the fruits of her labor after everything she had been through.

On my journey of following my relationship with God, I began attending church. I didn't immediately want to become a member because I was still discovering where this journey was taking me. I didn't want any interruptions. But I experienced unexpected interruptions, and I'm grateful for that.

As I typed this, I remembered watching those sermons. There would be moments when they would encourage viewers to manifest what they wanted, to ask God, claim it, and see it. One of the things I would say and claim was that I wanted a fiancé—a fiancé who would not divorce me, who would not be unfaithful, who would protect me. I yearned to experience love that was endless, unfailing, and unconditional, and I wanted to give that kind of love as well. I felt I had it in me, and I wanted to show someone special that love.

But I knew that on my own, I could never choose the right person for myself. So, I entrusted that responsibility to the One above, the all-knowing, wise God. I prayed about many things, but that main prayer was the one I longed for because I wanted to give my daughter a stable family.

By the time I was 22, I thought I was ready for a relationship. I felt a calling, but I couldn't understand what it was. In my mind, I thought it was ministry, so I made an appointment to meet with the pastor for advice on how to tackle it. But on my way there, I met someone—Vusi.

Initially, I was not keen on dating guys from the township. I had my own stereotypes based on what I had heard about boys from there, thinking they were all players, and I didn't want to be with someone from that background. Yet, despite having rejected many boys from the township, there was something different about him. Still, I needed confirmation; I couldn't just step into a relationship without being sure it was real and not just a fleeting attraction.

I just had to make sure I wasn't going to make the typical mistakes I had in the past, like falling for someone out of lust instead of love. I didn't want to find myself in the same situation again; I needed to be in a relationship that felt real and was not based solely on earthly desires.

I had basically fasted, tithed, prayed to God, and manifested that He would one day bless me with a fiancé. I was patiently waiting for that fiancé because I wanted someone I knew God would approve of—someone who understood me better than I did, since I had made mistakes before. I did not want to find myself in the same situation again, as it hadn't yielded any positive results in my life. It felt like I was taking steps back instead of healing.

As I embarked on this journey of healing, self-discovery, and building my relationship with God, I needed someone who would perfectly fit my new path, not distract me, or come between me and my relationship with God. I also wanted to avoid anyone who might trigger my past traumas. Although I desired all of this, I think I wasn't completely realistic. I expected my fiancé to be perfect, like someone walking straight out of a biblical story—barefoot like Moses, holding a staff, perhaps even leading a lamb.

I didn't anticipate that he would literally be right under my nose. I remember the first time I saw him; I couldn't stop staring. It felt like there was something magnetic drawing me to him. He stood in front of his gate, looking the other way, completely unaware of me. I stopped whatever I was doing and just looked at him, mesmerized, almost like a hungry baby wanting its mother's milk. I even had to call myself out for staring at someone I didn't even know, but there was something about him I couldn't ignore.

He lived next door, and every time his gate opened, I found myself peeking out the window to see if it was him. I couldn't understand what it was about this guy; it didn't feel the same as my usual crushes—this felt deeper, different. At that time, he had dreadlocks, and I didn't know much about him except for a few rumors, which made me skeptical about getting to know him. I preferred to admire him from a distance.

After being single for those years and raising my child, I focused on getting to know myself better and improving my relationship with God. I also went back to school, changing my major from accounting to business administration, all with my mother's guidance.

***

Chapter 7: A Divine Connection

As I immersed myself in my relationship with God, a profound shift began to take place within me. I found myself yearning for something deeper than earthly desires—a calling towards a life of spirituality and purpose. It was during this transformative period that the thought of dropping out of school to pursue a career in theology crossed my mind. It felt like a divine calling, a beckoning towards a path I was meant to follow. However, this idea was met with skepticism from my mother, who held the belief that those in ministry often faced uncertain futures.

In our conversation, she offered me an ultimatum: I could switch to business administration for the time being. Once I completed my degree, I could then explore theology. Though I sensed her reluctance to fully support my dreams, I appreciated her desire for me to have a safety net. So, I accepted her advice and enrolled in business administration. It was 2012, and after four years of navigating my studies—sometimes struggling, sometimes thriving—I began to find my footing.

One day in July, while walking to the shop, I felt a sudden jolt of recognition. I caught sight of him again, the man who had lingered in my thoughts. It had been two years since I first noticed him, and I had tried to move on, focusing instead on my studies and spiritual growth. Yet, there he was, standing in front of his gate, looking as striking as I remembered. When he greeted me, my heart raced with both excitement and trepidation.

"Can I join you for coffee sometime?" he asked, his casual demeanor surprising me. In a world where connections often felt fleeting and superficial, this genuine invitation felt like a promise of something deeper. Still, I hesitated. How could I let someone into my life when I had been so resolute about only allowing those chosen by God?

Weeks passed, and despite my best efforts to focus on my studies and raise my daughter, I found myself drawn back to thoughts of him. He lived next door, yet our paths rarely crossed. I was often consumed by chores, studying, and the strict routine my mother enforced. But the moments I did catch glimpses of him sent butterflies fluttering in my stomach.

I was in a delicate space, manifesting my dreams for a fiancé while deepening my relationship with God. My prayers were fervent, filled with hope for a future partner who would fit seamlessly into the life I envisioned—one built on faith and mutual respect.

My spiritual journey was blossoming. I found myself attending church more frequently, taking notes during sermons, and even exploring the depth of prayer. I began to pray in tongues, experiencing a profound connection that left me feeling both exhilarated and vulnerable. At times, I would lose track of time in prayer, overwhelmed by the presence of something greater than myself.

Then, just a day before I was to meet with my pastor to seek guidance on these spiritual awakenings, I saw him again. Dressed in formal attire, I could only think that perhaps he had just come from church. My heart raced as I wondered, could this be the answer to my prayers?

"Is this the man God has chosen for me?" I pondered. As our gazes met, I waved, feeling a thrill of possibility.

Fate smiled upon me. The very next day, while sitting outside with my daughter, I heard his gate creak open. My heart raced, a familiar flutter of excitement. This was it. I peeked outside, and there he was. Our brief conversation ignited something in me—his passion for God and his journey towards studying theology resonated deeply within me.

He shared with me his Rastafarian journey, explaining how it shaped his understanding of spirituality and community. "Rasta taught me to see the world through a lens of love and unity," he said, his eyes sparkling with passion. "It's not just a religion; it's a way of life." He spoke of the vibrant culture, the music, and the deep-rooted beliefs in the connection between humanity and the divine. He described the powerful sense of community, how Rastafarians support one another and strive for a world of equality and justice.

As he spoke, I felt a connection unlike any I had experienced before—a bond that felt woven by the hands of destiny. He had faced despair but emerged stronger, seeking to understand his Creator on a deeper level. His experiences of overcoming obstacles and finding solace in spirituality echoed my own journey.

We spent countless afternoons lost in conversation, exploring our beliefs and spirituality, and finding comfort in each other's company. Our discussions often meandered into the realms of faith and the complexities of life, but beneath it all lay an undeniable chemistry. We spoke of dreams, aspirations, and how our faith guided us through our individual paths. Each conversation brought us closer, unraveling layers of vulnerability and trust.

Then came the moment of revelation. During one of our late-night talks, he hesitated, and I could sense the weight of his words. "I think I'm developing feelings for you," he confessed, his eyes searching mine for understanding.

My heart swelled as I realized I felt the same. "I think I'm developing feelings for you too," I admitted, my voice barely above a whisper. The admission hung between us, charged with anticipation, the air thick with unspoken words.

As the days turned into weeks, our connection deepened. I prayed for clarity, for confirmation that this was indeed the path God had laid before me. Just when I needed it most, a message arrived—a long text from him, expressing how he had been praying for someone who would walk alongside him in faith.

In that moment, everything fell into place. This was the confirmation I had been seeking. He was the one I had prayed for, the man destined to be my partner. I felt a wave of peace wash over me, enveloping me in a warmth that assured me I was on the right path.

"God really does work in mysterious ways," I thought as I texted him back, "I love you too." Each word felt like a step toward the future we were meant to share, a commitment woven in faith and love.

Reflecting on that time, I realize how vital it was to embrace not only my spiritual journey but also the unexpected connections that God orchestrated in my life. This chapter was not just about finding love; it was about discovering myself and the power of faith intertwined with the beautiful chaos of human connection. As I stepped into this new chapter of my life, I felt empowered, ready to embrace the adventures ahead with God guiding our way.

***

Chapter 8: Between Tangibility and Spirit: The Fire Within

Unfortunately, our relationship was immediately met with challenges. It wasn't something that was automatically embraced, especially by my side of the family. I already had a child from a previous relationship, and things hadn't turned out the way my family had hoped. Perhaps, they weren't fully supportive of me having children by different men. The scrutiny I faced was something I couldn't control. I didn't have the power to dictate the kind of man he would be for me, or to the child we now had together.

What I did know, however, was that I wanted to give my child security, a loving home, a stable family—a father and a mother, both present. For me, blood didn't matter, DNA was irrelevant. Love was all that counted. They say "blood is thicker than water," but I believe spirit is thicker than blood. That's what happened in our case. Others might not have understood the bond that naturally developed between Vusi and my daughter, but it was something beyond control—something pure, something real.

No one taught my daughter to call Vusi "dad." One random day, when she was just three years old, she simply decided on her own to call him that. It was natural. It was automatic. And the connection between them was undeniable. At the time, Vusi believed he couldn't father children because of his experiences in previous relationships where he had never been able to conceive. For him, being blessed with the opportunity to be a father to my daughter was a gift—something he had longed for but never thought possible. He didn't force her to like him, nor did he impose himself into the tight bond I shared with my daughter. He entered into our lives naturally, in a way that made everything fit perfectly. It was meant to be, even if others couldn't see it at the time.

I knew in my heart that this was the path laid out for me. God had whispered it to me. This is why He had told me to leave the toxic relationship I was in before. This is why He had urged me to trust in Him. Everything seemed to fall into place quickly, and before I knew it, I was pregnant again. I found myself at a crossroads, having to choose between my future with Vusi, my daughter, the child I was carrying, and my family. My family didn't fully support my decision to have another child, and I was faced with the difficult choice of leaving home. I packed up my few belongings and, with my daughter in tow, I left.

I sought refuge at a women's shelter, knowing it was my responsibility to protect my children and provide for them, even if it meant making tough decisions. Vusi was hesitant, not wanting to come between me and my family, but I knew it was something I had to do. Looking back, I understand why my family felt the way they did—they were only trying to protect me. I can never hold a grudge for that. After all, they raised me and molded me into the woman I am today.

The time apart from my family allowed me to gain perspective. I realized that I wasn't just following the whims of new love—I was acting on something deeper. This was a calling, a path I knew I had to follow. I took a leap of faith, trusting that everything would work out. I believed that, in time, both of our families would reconcile, and that Vusi and I would build the life we dreamed of.

Living in the shelter wasn't easy. We were surrounded by women fleeing abusive relationships or struggling with their own hardships, and it was humbling to live off donated food. Vusi did what he could, bringing me clothes and other essentials, but life there was a struggle. The weight of my situation often overwhelmed me, especially knowing I was expecting a baby boy with the man I loved. Yet, the joy of that should have been overshadowed by the circumstances we were in.

One day, while at the shelter, I received a devastating phone call. My mother had become gravely ill after discovering I had left home. Her health had deteriorated rapidly, and guilt washed over me. It was then that I knew I had to make amends. I called her and apologized, not for leaving but for the pain my actions had caused. I assured her we were safe and that I had no ill feelings toward her. She, in turn, offered to come and take us home from the shelter.

When my mother arrived, the house mother of the shelter was elated for me. She knew how much I longed for reconciliation. During my time there, I had undergone counseling, and it helped me better understand my relationship with my mother. I knew she had always been protective of me, but at times, her protectiveness felt stifling. I was her only child, and the fear of losing me, especially as I ventured into starting my own family, had clouded her judgment.

My mother and I had always been close. She raised me after my father left, and we shared nearly everything. But as I grew older, her strict values became difficult for me to bear. I wasn't allowed to make mistakes, and the expectations she placed on me often left me feeling like I couldn't live my own life. When I was violated at the age of six, I couldn't bring myself to tell her. Fear of judgment kept me silent. These unspoken traumas created a wedge between us, one that we never fully addressed.

I often wonder if she expected me to reconcile with the father of my first child, despite the clear lack of fulfillment in that relationship. She couldn't see the good in Vusi the way I did. He was a man with aspirations, a deep sense of spirituality, and a good heart. Yet, the comparisons to my previous relationship clouded her judgment. She didn't approve of Vusi, not because of anything he had done, but because he didn't fit the mold of what she thought I needed.

Returning home, we tried to mend our relationship. But in our family, openly admitting wrongdoing isn't something that comes easily, especially for African mothers. The lack of accountability hindered our progress, and while we never fully healed from our differences, I made a conscious choice to forgive. Not just my mother, but also myself.

This decision to forgive was influenced by my relationship with God and the sense that I had a calling. Although it's hard to sit and know you have a calling but can't even fulfill it. Some people may not really think highly of it. Sometimes, it makes you think: maybe I'm crazy, maybe I'm losing my mind, maybe these people are right—I don't know. So, you end up not knowing what to do. You seek answers, you cry at night by yourself because you just don't know what to do. And it doesn't help when you constantly have these episodes of being overcome and overwhelmed by this great feeling, like there's something in you that wants to come out—it's like a burning fire—and you just want to let it out. But you can't. You have to suppress it because you might be judged, you might not be understood, and it might not be received well.

People—humanity—don't easily accept these kinds of things because we are too focused on living in the physical. Whatever we can see with the physical eye is what matters the most. It's not always easy for us to fully dive into spirituality and understand it, to understand that in as much as we live in the physical world, we are also spiritual beings. And sometimes the spirit gets thirsty, it gets hungry. That's how I used to feel—that my spirit was thirsty, that my spirit was hungry. As much as I was feeding my physical body, I just couldn't get the fulfillment. I would still feel hungry spiritually.

How do you feed your spirit if you live in a space that doesn't really allow you to do so freely? You're always overcome by emotions; you cry alone, you pray, you listen to spiritual music, and you lift yourself up again. But most of the time, you feel alone. I don't know if you know the feeling of what it's like to feel like you're the only person in the world who thinks and feels like this. It's so rare to find a person who thinks, feels, talks, and believes like you. That was my reality.

I think this is the moment where you have to pick between tangible and intangible. What's more meaningful? Is it really what we can see, or is it what we cannot see but can feel—and it makes us feel fulfilled, even though it's not tangible? If it's tangible, but when I "eat" it, it still doesn't fulfill me, then what's the point? Tangibility is just that—because it's physical and we can see and touch it. But maybe what's greater and bigger is what we cannot comprehend. That's what we cannot see.

Who is the Creator? We cannot see the Creator; we cannot touch the Creator, but we can feel the Creator. So many religions believe in the concept of a Creator, yet no one can attest to having physically seen Him. But the way that belief makes you feel is magnificent. It becomes a feeling you become almost addicted to, and you don't want to let it go—it's like breath itself, it's life. At some point, you feel like death is nothing. You feel like maybe there's more life in death than in life itself.

Sometimes life feels like death. Sometimes life feels like a slumber you are not waking up from, because every day, it's the same: "I cannot believe this is happening; I cannot believe this is happening to me." But when that moment of crossing over or separating from the physical body happens, would you be shocked? I don't know. But again, who does?

We go around seeking.

***

Chapter 9: Holding On Through the Storm

All the challenges we were facing, and growing our family, seemed to bring us closer. I breathed easier with each day that passed, as Vusi and I drew closer. Despite the difficulties, we spent those two years focusing on growing together, completing our degrees, and raising our children. Then, after two years, Vusi asked me to marry him. It wasn't the typical knee-on-the-ground, ring-in-hand proposal. Instead, in true African fashion, Vusi simply said, "I was thinking of sending my delegates to speak to your family and negotiate lobola." That was it—direct and straightforward. No grand gestures, just a man telling me he was ready to take the next step. And with that, I said yes, deeply moved by his intention. By then, we had been together for two years. Both of us were working, things were looking good, and my family had started to accept him. Our relationship was growing stronger, and I was excited about the new adventure ahead. Our two children were growing, and life felt more stable and happy. Sealing that bond with marriage just felt right.

But what Vusi didn't know was that I was afraid—terrified, actually. I came from a home of divorced parents, and marriage scared the living daylights out of me. I thought I was destined to fail. I didn't want to get married only to end up divorced, but I also couldn't picture a future without him. When you're not married, it's easy to brush off little issues or avoid deep arguments. If something bothered me, I'd sweep it under the rug, hoping it would go away. I wondered if we got along too well, considering we hadn't had any serious arguments in two years. It seemed impossible, almost unreal.

In January 2014, Vusi sent his delegates to my family for the first lobola negotiations, and we were officially engaged. This news wasn't met with overwhelming joy from my family. In our culture, a mother often feels like she's losing her daughter when she marries and joins another family. My mother, being alone, feared being left behind. I tried my best to reassure her that I would always be there for her, no matter what.

We didn't set a wedding date immediately because the negotiations weren't finalized. We continued living together, raising our children, working, and sacrificing. But as our family grew, life became more serious. Financial pressures started to weigh heavily on us. Sometimes, we were both working, but at other times, we weren't. These shifts put a strain on us, especially since we needed to provide for our children without asking for help from our parents or anyone else. We did everything we could to make ends meet.

At one point, I started working in sales and did exceptionally well, increasing the company's profits by 80%. But I hadn't realized how this success would affect Vusi. He was unemployed at the time, having lost his job at the university. It hurt his ego, though he never said it directly. The tension between us simmered silently. Vusi had just lost his dream job—working in the Department of Systematic Theology at the university. His contract wasn't renewed, and it shattered him. It took years for him to recover from that loss. He had studied for that job, aligned his career with it, and suddenly, it was gone. But he didn't talk about it. I don't know what it is about African men, but many keep their emotions buried deep inside.

Vusi wasn't a vocal person, and although this frustrated me, I tried to understand him. He wasn't one to openly express his feelings, but I could see the weight of his pain in his eyes. It broke my heart. He looked like he was dying inside, wanting to scream but afraid of being judged or seen as weak. Vusi grew up without a father, having lost his father when he was just 16. He had to find father figures in the streets, where not all the examples were good ones. Some were gang members; others were men who didn't set great examples, and this had a profound impact on him.

I tried to keep everything together. I had been raised to be strong, and I couldn't let our family sink. Vusi was going through a rough time, and I had to be the strong one for him. We both worked at the same university at one point, but after my contract was renewed for the second year and eventually ended, I moved into sales while Vusi remained unemployed.

During his unemployment, we decided to start a school transportation business using our small 2008 Hyundai Getz. It wasn't much, but it helped bring in a little income. Though it wasn't enough, it was something. I was working on commission, which made life tough, but I still managed to make sales. However, it didn't put us in the financial position we desired. We had big dreams—owning a farm, starting a church, and me opening a private school—but these dreams felt so distant. It seemed like we were moving backward instead of forward.

With a growing family of five at this time to support, we did everything we could to provide. We paid school fees, covered transportation for the kids, ensured we had food, and kept gas in the car so we could work or transport the children. Life was difficult, but looking back now, we were a good team. We worked together through everything, even as Vusi silently drowned in sorrow. As a man, he wanted to be the provider, but that role kept slipping through his fingers. He wasn't reaching the place he had envisioned for us—having a house, working, being settled. I believe he had a plan: after paying lobola, we would get married, live in our own home, and everything would fall into place. But life had other plans, and seeing him struggle like that broke me.

It was hard to watch the man I loved go through so much pain.

***

Chapter 10: Shifting Sands: A Journey of Understanding

In 2018, Vusi finally secured a permanent job at a prestigious company. He had been searching for stability for what felt like an eternity, and when this opportunity arose, it seemed like an enormous blessing. He began thriving in the role, and it felt as though the weight of financial pressure had finally lifted. With his new job, we could afford our basic standard of living again. It was a period of immense relief for me—I could breathe again. But as with many seasons in life, this peace was fleeting. What I had hoped would be a lasting reprieve soon took an unexpected turn.

Vusi's new job, while a blessing in many ways, came with its own set of challenges. The position demanded more from him than any of us anticipated. His work began consuming most of his time, and he was no longer home as much as he used to be. Long hours turned into late nights, and soon, his job started to take a toll—not just on him, but on our family. The pressure to perform, to secure his position in the company, was overwhelming him. He became consumed with proving his worth, desperate to cement his place in the company and ensure our financial future. Unfortunately, that desperation led him to make decisions that would ultimately cost him his job.

At that time, I was running my own aftercare business, a venture I had started out of a passion for working with young people. I helped learners with their homework, tutoring them in subjects like mathematics, English, and accounting. The business was doing well, and for the first time in years, we had two steady incomes—one from Vusi's job and one from my business. With four children to care for at this point, this financial stability felt like a dream come true. We both wanted a big family; having grown up as an only child raised by my mother, I wanted to experience having a large family. He grew up with four other siblings and, because he enjoyed being in a big family, he wanted the same thing. I dared to hope, imagining a future where our hard work would finally pay off. But life, as it often does, threw us a curveball.

One afternoon, I received a phone call from Vusi while he was still at work. His voice was quiet, filled with a hesitation I hadn't heard in years. He told me that he had been fired. I stood there, stunned, unable to respond. Fear, confusion, and uncertainty washed over me. How were we going to manage? With three children in school and one small baby, we needed more than just a little money to get by. Our financial needs were significant, and with only one income—my business income—I wasn't sure how we'd survive. The security I had felt only moments before seemed to vanish.

Running a business while raising children is no small feat. The demands are constant, the work never-ending. Now, with Vusi out of a job, I found myself feeling overwhelmed and uncertain. How were we going to provide for our family with only a single income? On top of the financial strain, I felt a deep sense of shame. I couldn't be honest with my family about why Vusi had lost his job. His decisions seemed reckless, and I was embarrassed to admit that we were struggling because of these poor decisions. I felt isolated, carrying the burden alone, and soon resentment started creeping into my heart.

As I wrestled with these emotions, I embarked on a journey of forgiveness. Forgiving Vusi was not easy, but in doing so, I learned to see him—and men in general—in a different light. Society often overlooks the role men play in their families. Women, especially mothers, are celebrated for their nurturing, for their ability to balance the needs of the home and children. But men, too, carry heavy burdens. They face pressures we sometimes don't acknowledge, and their struggles are just as valid as ours.

Men work in environments that are physically and emotionally demanding. Industries like oil drilling, construction, and mining are fraught with danger. Men endure harsh conditions, long hours, and physical strain, often far from their families. Yet, this work, which many women—including myself—would find nearly impossible, goes largely unrecognized. On the other hand, women bring their own unique strengths to the family dynamic—qualities like patience, empathy, and resilience. Both roles are essential, and neither should be diminished.

Childbirth is an example of the unique challenges women face. Having given birth to five children, I can attest to the physical and emotional toll it takes. The hormonal changes, the physical pain, and the exhaustion are overwhelming. After my first child, I experienced postpartum depression. I felt anxious, overwhelmed, and lost. My body had changed, and the weight gain left me vulnerable to hurtful comments and body-shaming. I had always prided myself on being strong, but in that period, I felt anything but strong.

Raising children requires every ounce of your energy and love. It's not just about ensuring they're fed or dressed—it's about nurturing their souls, guiding them through life's ups and downs, and being present for them even when you're utterly exhausted. Yet, society often diminishes the importance of this work, especially if you're a stay-at-home mother. It's as if the absence of a paycheck makes your work invisible, when in fact, nothing could be further from the truth.

Having a partner who recognizes and values your contribution can make all the difference. I had to learn to see Vusi's role as the provider with more empathy. The pressure he felt to succeed was immense, and it was only after his job loss that I began to understand just how much weight he had been carrying. This realization didn't come easily. It required me to step back and reflect on the dynamics of our relationship and the societal expectations that weigh heavily on both men and women.

I found myself thinking about the story of Adam and Eve in the Bible. When God told Adam that he would labor for the rest of his life, we often overlook the gravity of that statement. Men are expected to provide, to be strong, to handle adversity without faltering. But is it really fair to place such heavy expectations on them? Society has conditioned us to believe that men should be able to handle anything because "they're men." But the reality is, they're human, too.

In the same way, God told Eve that she would suffer the pain of childbirth. I've always found that statement to be a profound reflection of the burden women carry. Childbirth is not something that can be endured easily, and yet women go through it, sometimes multiple times, with grace and strength. Similarly, men's labor—whether physical or emotional—deserves the same respect. Both forms of labor are grueling, and neither should be taken lightly.

For a long time, I believed my role as a mother was more important than Vusi's role as a provider. I was giving life, nurturing our children, raising them into the world. Surely, that was the most important work. But as I watched Vusi grapple with the loss of his job, I began to see things differently. His role as a provider was just as crucial as my role as a nurturer. We needed each other, and that realization brought me a newfound appreciation for him.

Before I met Vusi, I had unrealistic expectations of what a fiancé should be. I envisioned a Moses or Abraham-like figure, someone who had walked all the way from Jerusalem, barefoot and holding a staff, leading with wisdom and strength. I believed a godly man would have no flaws, no struggles, and I thought I had worked through all my own imperfections to deserve such a man. But reality was far more complex. Neither of us was perfect, and that's okay. What mattered was our commitment to each other and to our family.

Being a single mother before I met Vusi had its own set of challenges. My family helped raise my first child, but it was exhausting—physically, emotionally, and mentally. There were no breaks, no time off. Having a partner to share that load makes a world of difference. For years, Vusi and I had been a team, and even though we didn't always agree or see eye to eye, we were in it together. Imagining losing that sense of partnership, even temporarily, was a painful reminder of how much I valued his presence.

Vusi, too, had learned the value of partnership during the four years he was single, just before we met. He had come to understand that he needed a wife just as much as I needed a fiancé. Society often glorifies independence, pushing the narrative that needing someone is a weakness. But I've come to realize that we were designed to need each other. We were made to build each other up, to support each other in times of need.

Partnership is not about one person being more important than the other. It's about recognizing that both people have their own battles to fight, their own roles to play, and that neither should be diminished. When we stop comparing ourselves to each other, when we stop trying to "fix" each other, we can create a stronger, more loving bond. In marriage, as in life, it's the recognition of each other's worth that sustains us.

There is no perfect formula for how a household should function. Some men prefer to be in the kitchen, while others avoid it. Some women excel at parenting, while others struggle. It's about finding what works for each couple and building a partnership based on mutual respect and love. In the end, we all bring our own strengths to the table, and it's these differences that make us stronger together.

***

Chapter 11: Awakening The Truth

I was utterly unprepared for the myriad changes and challenges that came with our relationship. I realized too late that I had committed myself only to the good times, neglecting the terrible, sleepless nights filled with heart-wrenching conversations, tears, and frustration. I hadn't braced myself for the moments when he would feel disconnected, burdened by the weight of our financial struggles.

You see, my fiancé was raised with a deeply ingrained belief that a man is the provider, a notion that became problematic when opportunities for me to work arose. He would never voice his feelings, but I could see it in his eyes—the discomfort that flickered whenever I contributed to our family's expenses. Paying school fees, buying food, and shouldering the financial responsibilities began to weigh heavily on him. At first, I tried to reassure him that our dynamic wouldn't change our bond. I believed we could balance things—he would care for the children while I worked, and I would take over once I returned home. But as time passed, this delicate balance unraveled, leading us into uncharted territory.

After ten long years together, he still hadn't completed his lobola, leaving us in a state of unofficial union. We were raising four beautiful children, and I was pregnant with our fifth when COVID struck, hitting us like a ton of bricks. He had taken a job at a different company, but our finances barely stretched to meet our needs. We couldn't afford our own place, which forced us to move in with my mother. This arrangement was incredibly challenging, as I knew I needed him by my side. Managing our children alone—while pregnant, homeschooling, running an aftercare business, and grappling with my spiritual journey—felt like an insurmountable task.

This chapter of my life unfolded when I least expected it. I thought my relationship with God was solid; I had read the entire Bible, prayed fervently, and raised my children under His word. Yet, everything began to shift dramatically.

During my pregnancy, I fell ill, and I was unsure of what was happening to my body. Our first instinct was to test for pregnancy, but three separate tests came back negative. Deep down, I knew something was wrong, though I couldn't pinpoint it. For years, I had struggled with itchy ears, persistent bloating, blurry visions, and stomach issues that never seemed to fade. I underwent countless tests—a colonoscopy, blood tests, ultrasounds—but each result returned negative, leaving me feeling more frustrated and lost. I could sense my body deteriorating, but without answers, I felt helpless. My dreams became more vivid, haunted by a terrible backache that made it difficult to function. It felt as though my entire being was surrendering to an unknown force.

I never anticipated embarking on a spiritual journey, especially not in such a tumultuous way. In African culture, there are many divine healers, bone readers, and seers. I used to fear these individuals because I didn't understand their world. There's a stigma surrounding them, a belief that they are possessed or worship dark spirits. Yet, I found myself inexplicably drawn to these spiritual matters, having strange dreams where I envisioned helping others. Confusion enveloped me; I had no answers, and those around me seemed equally lost.

As if that weren't enough, my fiancé embarked on his own journey of self-discovery, seeking deeper answers in spirituality. This path ultimately led us to step away from the church and the community we had known. We were besieged by a cascade of changes—COVID, financial strain, and a multitude of life challenges crashing over us like relentless waves. We felt overwhelmed and unprepared for the storm that had suddenly engulfed our lives.

One thing I knew for certain was that I was deeply terrified. I looked at my children and couldn't imagine leaving them while they were so young. I needed to find a way to heal. When we visited a seer, I discovered that I had a spiritual calling. The signs had always been there, yet I had never truly understood what they meant. My family, on the other hand, was not immediately convinced; there was a lot of skepticism. But here I was, feeling as though I was losing my life and needing to do whatever it took to save it.

I decided to go to initiation school because the answers I sought from my family felt elusive, as if I were speaking a foreign language. The truth is, I too felt this was completely unfamiliar territory. Yet the strength of my inner conviction was undeniable. Despite my previous skepticism, it seemed I had no choice but to embrace this path. My body was getting weaker.

Throughout this journey, my fiancé was by my side. He provided me with everything I needed. If I had a dream or vision that guided me to pray at the river or on the mountain, he was there, ensuring I woke up on time and taking care of me as I navigated my journey. I didn't fully understand what I was doing, but we followed every instinct I felt compelled to pursue. We would rise early in the morning to pray by the river.

This was during winter, and it was freezing. We later discovered that we were expecting another child while also going through this difficult time. Most of my warm clothes no longer fit as my pregnancy progressed, so I would wrap myself in a blanket while wearing what could still fit to stay warm and keep the baby cozy. You can imagine the challenge of climbing a mountain while pregnant or walking to the river through uncomfortable terrain. Many areas in the townships and city are not designed to accommodate the spiritual needs of African culture, making it difficult to find accessible places to reach a river or mountain without paying a fee, especially given our limited income at the time.

Doing all the things made me steadily get better physically. I was beginning to regain my strength slowly, but the dreams and visions were getting more and more intense. At this point, my mother was also beginning to have dreams, and I believe this was a way to confirm for both of us that this was truly not just in my imagination—that it was real.

My mother decided to help me get the answers I needed as I was about to leave for initiation school the next day. She advised that we see another seer.

During the divination, I was advised that this journey did not require me to go to initiation school to embrace my path and seek answers; instead, I just needed to be patient, pray, and meditate consistently, and my guides would reveal themselves to me as they had been doing through dreams and visions. I began to now believe that this was real. It changed the way I thought about such things. I realized at this point that we were really misinformed as Black Africans about who we truly are. Sometimes, religion can take away from what we truly are if we misinterpret the teachings. Sometimes we want to read the Bible to fit what we want and not fully grasp the message with understanding.

As I was embarking on this journey, I was finding a lot of my answers in the same Bible—how to perform certain ceremonies to cleanse my aura and connect deeper with my guides. I was beginning to understand why I had this gift of praying in tongues because this is what I was consistently doing throughout this journey. There were moments when I couldn't even pray in my own language because I was consumed by this great force, and I would let it guide me and teach me how to pray. I felt like I was connecting with my Creator in a much deeper way, but this time I was acknowledging that He wasn't walking and working alone. I had always had these guides surrounding me, but I had thought I was imagining things.

From the time I was in primary school and saw the spirit of the young girl who had passed away, to being filled with such a great spirit that taught me how to pray in tongues, my whole curiosity about faith, the Creator, and how everything works was growing. I was being drawn to nature and everything beyond. It was all beginning to make sense. It was like all the pieces of the puzzle were now coming together. I felt whole for the first time, and I was grateful to have my fiancé by my side.

***

Chapter 12: Embracing The Call

I was embarking on a journey that many may find unsettling, often feeling overwhelmingly scary. Confronted with this reality, I realized that I could no longer live solely focused on my individual goals and dreams. I needed to embrace a life of servanthood, dedicating myself to serving others. This shift in perspective was profound and transformative, revealing layers of purpose I had yet to understand fully.

There was a time when I felt a deep calling—a profound pull toward ministry that resonated in my soul. It felt like a deep-rooted truth, beckoning me to step into a role I had never anticipated. At that point, I was willing to leave my university course behind to study theology, driven by an intense longing. However, that chapter of my life was unexpectedly interrupted; it wasn't received with open arms. This interruption caused me to lose focus, leading to confusion and doubt.

Life can be relentless, and your calling will always find you. Even if you try to escape or seek different paths, your calling will disrupt your life, bringing everything to a standstill. In those moments, your only choice is to stop and listen. Sometimes, these interruptions manifest through losing your job, struggling financially, or facing issues in your marriage or with your children. The loss of a loved one can also serve as a wake-up call, urging you to confront what you've been running away from.

In our fast-paced lives, distractions abound, pulling us away from our true selves. We often strive to meet the expectations of others, losing sight of our essence in the process. This distraction led to a profound sense of loss, as I forgot the reasons for my existence.

The greatest interruption in my life came when illness consumed me, confining me to my bed in pain. Pregnant and unable to care for my other children, I had to rely heavily on family. My fiancé had to shoulder more responsibility, which was difficult for me; I had always prided myself on being in control, feeling like a superwoman. Yet, during this time, I realized I was failing to appreciate my life. I was losing myself and my sense of direction. Though I still believed in God and prayed consistently, I wasn't fully living my purpose, leaving me lost and uncertain.

Often, I found myself crying, overwhelmed by emotions that trapped me in a cycle of despair. I had to turn inward and reflect on what I had missed. It was then that I began to listen to the voices within me, which I had drowned out with life's chaos. The noise of everyday life can be deafening; we become inundated with music, news, work, and social events that disconnect us from our true selves.

In moments of isolation, even surrounded by loved ones, I felt as if I were in my own world. My experiences were often too complex to articulate, making it hard for others to relate. I yearned for solitude, straining my relationships. I didn't want my fiancé to feel unloved or unwanted, but I couldn't suppress the urge to retreat. This burden felt too heavy to share, and the weight of it became overwhelming.

This struggle took a toll on my relationships. I pushed my fiancé away, fearing he would see my vulnerability, yet this created distance between us. He, being patient and understanding, tried to navigate this challenging time with me. Watching me suffer, he remained steadfast, even as I grew frustrated with myself for needing help. I had to confront my dependency on others, which felt alien. There were moments when I would push people away, only to realize later that I needed assistance—whether it was to go to the bathroom or simply to eat.

I became acutely aware of how essential my support system was; my mother and fiancé became my pillars of strength, offering empathy even when they couldn't fully grasp my struggle. Their presence was invaluable, reminding me that I wasn't alone in this battle. They stood by me, providing encouragement during my darkest moments, even when I struggled to articulate my feelings. It was a bittersweet realization, knowing I needed them while feeling burdened by my situation.

This journey of healing lasted nearly two years, marked by a cycle of wellness and illness. I gave birth during this time and continued to grapple with my health. The fluctuations of my physical condition mirrored my emotional state. Friends prayed for me, and I sought help from those who had faced similar challenges. Their support was invaluable. In moments of desperation, prayer became my refuge, bringing calmness and reconnection to reality.

As I healed, I began to recognize that my struggles were not purely physical; they were deeply spiritual. I learned that one can suffer spiritually as profoundly as one can physically. Even amidst relative stability—my fiancé's love and my children's well-being—I felt overwhelmed by a spiritual hunger I couldn't articulate. I realized I was seeking something beyond mere relief from my physical pain; I was searching for deeper meaning and a connection to my true self.

After two years, I sought help from healers who employed methods beyond modern medicine. These healers possessed a wealth of knowledge about holistic approaches to well-being, recognizing that the body, mind, and spirit are interconnected. Through their guidance, I gradually reclaimed my strength. I discovered healing in worship, in the rhythm of drums, and in dance. There was liberation in expressing myself in ways I had never explored before, allowing my spirit to soar.

This journey revealed unexpected gifts within me, as I realized I was meant to help heal others through prayer and connection. This realization was both empowering and humbling. It became evident that my experiences were not just for my own benefit but were meant to prepare me to help others who might find themselves in similar pain. I learned that true understanding comes from shared experiences; you cannot genuinely help those in need unless you've walked a similar path.

Through this process, I began to embrace the vulnerability that had once felt burdensome. I understood that sharing my story could empower others. The struggles I faced resonated with many who silently battled their demons. My journey of healing transformed into one of service, as I sought to extend a hand to those in need.

This journey has illuminated the depth of spirituality that often goes unacknowledged. We are more than our physical selves; we are beings of spirit, craving connection, understanding, and purpose. In our quest for the tangible, we can forget the richness of our spiritual existence. I've come to embrace this journey, knowing that every struggle has brought me closer to my true self and my calling.

I am rediscovering parts of myself that had been buried beneath layers of pain and obligation. Each beat of the drum resonated with my heartbeat, creating a connection that transcended words. Dance became a language of its own, a way to express emotions I had long suppressed. In those moments of movement, I felt liberated and alive, a stark contrast to the confinement of illness.

The deeper I delved into my own healing, the clearer it became that my journey intertwined with the experiences of countless others. I began to embrace the vulnerability that had once felt burdensome. Sharing my story became a source of strength, revealing that the struggles I faced were not just mine; they resonated with many, quietly battling their demons.

Each connection I made with others reinforced the notion that we are part of a larger tapestry of human experience. Reflecting on this time in my life, I see how vital it was to learn the art of surrender. Letting go of the need to control everything opened new avenues for growth and healing. I learned to trust the process, even when it felt uncertain. In those moments of surrender, I found clarity, understanding that my journey was not a linear path but a beautiful tapestry woven with both light and dark threads.

As I navigate life now, I carry the lessons of resilience, empathy, and connection with me. Each day is an opportunity to live out my calling and serve others in meaningful ways. I've learned to listen deeply, offer support without judgment, and create spaces where others feel safe to share their stories. This calling is a responsibility I embrace with humility, recognizing that I am merely a vessel for something greater.

I also find joy in small moments—those simple acts of kindness that can change someone's day. Whether it's a warm smile, a listening ear, or a helping hand, I've come to understand that these gestures have the power to uplift and heal. In serving others, I rediscover pieces of myself that I had lost along the way. It's a beautiful cycle of giving and receiving, where both parties walk away enriched by the experience.

This journey has taught me the importance of self-care. To be truly present for others, I must first nurture my well-being, allowing moments of rest, reflection, and rejuvenation. It's a delicate balance, but one I am committed to maintaining. I recognize that I cannot pour from an empty cup; I must ensure that I am replenished to continue serving those around me.

As I continue to explore the depths of my calling, I am constantly reminded of the interconnectedness of all beings. Each person I encounter carries their own story, struggles, and triumphs. It's this shared humanity that binds us together, reminding me that we are never truly alone. Navigating this complex tapestry of life reveals beauty and opportunity within that complexity.

I embrace the journey ahead with an open heart and a willing spirit. I know there will be challenges, but I also believe that each challenge presents an opportunity for growth. I am committed to staying true to my purpose, listening to the whispers of my calling, and remaining attuned to the needs of those around me. Together, we can create a world filled with understanding, compassion, and healing.

This journey is not just mine; it's a shared experience that connects us all. I am grateful for every twist and turn, every moment of struggle, and every victory along the way. In the end, our stories define us, and I am ready to embrace mine fully.

***

Conclusion: Embracing New Beginnings: A Journey of Healing and Hope

This is my last chapter for this part of my life. It concludes with us having set the wedding date. After years and months of finding different ways of healing (by tapping into spirituality) and allowing the body to address trivial trauma, you know, when I was going through this experience of healing, my body would tremble a lot, and I could feel that it was the trauma within me. After having used those rhythms of the drum and the vibrations to heal what was within and essentially heal my body, I feel like a new person again. I'm at a point where I now have a better and stronger relationship with my mother. Even though I lost my father along the way, I'm happy that it happened at a time when we found the space to really talk about what happened between us, and I was able to forgive him. I was in a space where I could see and understand better, and I think I'm okay now. I miss my dad every day; I see him in my dreams, obviously, and I do believe he's still with me spiritually. I love him dearly, and I will always love him. I embrace this moment because, without all of these people in my life, this book wouldn't even have been possible.

I tell these stories because of the impact that these different people have made in my life. I also want to dedicate this book to my teachers, especially to those who made an impact in my life because, somehow, they made me see myself with different eyes. You know, things that I didn't believe in myself. My other name is Pride, and there was a teacher of mine who used to call me the "Pride of the Nation." At that point, I did not understand why she gave me such a big title, but I think now it's not just about wanting to be the pride of the nation but to be the pride of yourself and to be proud of yourself first before you can want other people to be proud of you. I live today proud of myself for having converted my journey and for having survived even the most dreadful experiences. I sought counseling to find healing; this really helped me and allowed me to see myself in a different light and not think of myself as a victim but as a victor. Today, I stand here with only these stories to tell and a lot of great memories to share. I tell my children a lot about my life experiences, and it's the first time that I put it on paper where they can read about it. I want to share this part of my life with people in the hopes that it will make a difference.

We now have five healthy children together; we finally set a date for our wedding, and the wedding planning is going very well. I hope that in my next book, I will tell you about how that is going. I cannot wait to spend the rest of my life with a man who's been with me through the most difficult times of my life, who helped me to grieve my father. He was there through every experience. He was there for my first graduation, and he was there when I had our children. He has always been there; he has never left my side, and he's always been there. I call him "Chommie," which means my friend because, truly, he's my best friend. I feel like he's another person who understands me a lot, and I feel like he's more patient with me than I am with myself. Sometimes, I put a lot of pressure on myself, and he's the one who calms me down and says, "*No, you don't always have to be overwhelmed; you don't always have to overthink things; you can take one thing at a time.*" He's definitely the one to take things one step at a time, even though sometimes it frustrates me, and I become impatient with him, asking him why he waits or why he procrastinates. But maybe procrastination is not always a bad thing. Sometimes, we do need to take the time to reflect before we take a step. Sometimes, maybe it does help us avoid mistakes, but I think that's how we balance each other.

In moments where he's afraid to take a step, I'm the one who is ahead and says, "*Okay, let me start this and show you that it's possible.*" I just see him follow after, and he then takes over. He's the executor. I plan a lot of things in our relationship, but I think because I'm more reserved, he somehow is able to do the things that I would plan and say, and then he executes them. Having a partner like that has really helped me a lot in life. He's my prayer partner; we pray a lot together. It's not always perfect; sometimes life does get in the way, and we forget to pray. But we always come back and remind each other why it's important to always be connected to God. I'm grateful for my journey.

I'm grateful that I'm in a space where today people ask me for help and advice in terms of spiritual guidance, and I try to allow my guides to help them as best as I can. I'm also still a student on this journey; I don't know everything. I'm still learning myself, but I'm glad that I get to share the knowledge that I have been able to gather.

I'm grateful to my mother for always being the woman I look up to; she inspires me a lot. Having gone through all the things she went through herself, today she's a doctor. She comes from a divorced marriage, but that did not define her. I think she herself has a lot of people to be grateful for. I'm grateful for my uncles. My elder uncle's teachings; even though he raised us in a very strict manner, I think I wouldn't have been this headstrong if those advisors and teachings were not there. Yes, we are not perfect, and sometimes we all need healing. But I think that we all make an impact on people's lives that sometimes we're not even aware of—how much we lift them up in their lives.

For me, a lot of people left a mark on me. My grandmother also inspires me every day because she's such a strong woman. But even in her strength, sometimes you can see that vulnerability, and you know that even the strongest people also get vulnerable sometimes, and they too need people to hold them and stand by them. She's getting older now, and of course, I cannot imagine life without her because it's almost like I see life through her. She inspires me to fight, you know, and I'm grateful to be surrounded by such wonderful women. Today, I hold my bachelor's in business administration. Together with my fiancé, we are running this business. It's been 12 years of being together facing our ups and downs, and we are slowly but steadily finding our way financially. We're not there yet, but we strive every day to get to where we want to be. We have started our own church, with the support of our families, and we are raising our children under the word of God while also embracing our gifts and always acknowledging our guides. We remember that we wouldn't exist, and we wouldn't be who we are if our ancestors did not exist, and every day we acknowledge them.

It is not about worshipping because you cannot worship another human being, but you can acknowledge, honor, and be grateful for the impact that they made in your life. This is what we love to do. I cannot know myself if I don't know where I come from because without these people, I do not exist. It's a bloodline that I will forever be proud of, from both my father's DNA that is within me. I am proud to be who I am.

As I sit here reflecting on my life, I can't help but feel a profound sense of gratitude for the path I've traveled. This memoir has been more than just a collection of stories; it has been a way to honor my experiences and the people who shaped me. Each chapter represents a milestone, a lesson learned, and a moment of resilience. It's a testament to the strength that comes from vulnerability and the healing power of sharing one's truth.

I think back to the struggles that once seemed insurmountable. There were days when the weight of my past felt like an anchor, pulling me down. Yet, with every challenge, I found a way to rise. Through counseling, spirituality, and the unwavering support of my loved ones, I learned to transform pain into purpose. I discovered that healing is not a destination but a continuous journey, one that requires patience and compassion for oneself.

My children often ask me about my experiences, eager to understand the woman they see before them. I share stories of resilience, of the times I felt lost but found my way back, not just for them but for myself as well. I want them to know that life is filled with highs and lows, but it's how we navigate those moments that truly defines us. I want them to embrace their emotions, to know it's okay to feel, to grieve, and to celebrate.

As I prepare for this next chapter in my life—our wedding—I'm reminded of the beauty of new beginnings. Love has a way of renewing the spirit, of igniting hope even in the darkest of times. My fiancé, my *Chommie*, has been my anchor, standing by my side as I faced my demons. Together, we have built a foundation of trust, understanding, and love. I look forward to weaving our lives together even more, to creating a home filled with laughter, faith, and the kind of love that transcends adversity.

I envision a future where our children not only learn from my experiences but also carve their own paths, unencumbered by the weight of the past. I hope to nurture their dreams, to encourage them to chase their passions, and to stand firm in their beliefs. I want them to know that they have the power to create their own stories, just as I have done.

In the years to come, I aspire to be a voice for others who may be struggling. I want to share my journey in a way that inspires hope and encourages healing. Whether through writing, speaking, or mentoring, I feel a calling to support those navigating their own storms. I believe that our stories hold the power to connect us, to remind us that we are not alone in our struggles.

As I close this chapter, I hold onto the lessons learned, the love shared, and the strength gained. I look to the future with optimism, ready to embrace whatever comes my way. I know there will be challenges, but I am no longer afraid. I have built a toolkit of resilience, surrounded by a community of love and support.

This is not just an ending; it is a new beginning. I step into the next phase of my life with an open heart, ready to create new memories, share new experiences, and continue growing. I am proud of who I am and where I come from, and I look forward to the legacy I will leave behind—not just in written words but in the lives I touch.

So, as I close this chapter of my life, I hear the gentle whisper once again, the one that has been with me through every step, and it says, "*You are mine."* Forever. Whether it is God, my internal voice, my guides or whatever it is, I'm grateful for it.

Thank you for being part of my journey.

***

About the Author

Danisile Skhosana, writing under the pen name *Pride Nthabiseng Matjila-Zwane*, is a passionate storyteller and devoted mother, wife, and entrepreneur. With a Bachelor of Business Administration and years of experience in education, Danisile has always been driven by the desire to inspire others through her personal journey.

Her memoir, *You Are Mine*, is a deeply personal reflection on her life, filled with the lessons she has learned from her family, faith, and experiences. Through her writing, she shares the story of discovering her identity, embracing her purpose, and understanding the transformative power of love—both for herself and for those closest to her.

Danisile's story is one of resilience, perseverance, and the belief that every moment in life holds a lesson. She is the founder of Azania Educational Services and Transportation, a company dedicated to providing support to learners in low-income communities. When not writing or running her business, Danisile is actively engaged in homeschooling her children, creating space for personal growth, and working toward expanding her online school.

Danisile's work, both as an author and an educator, is rooted in the belief that love, faith, and the courage to share our stories can change lives.